I0759895

Amy Lowell

illustrated by

Paolo Domeniconi

Climbing

Creative Editions

High up in the apple tree
climbing I go,

With the sky above me,
the earth below.

Each branch is the step of a wonderful stair
Which leads to the town I see shining up there.

Climbing, climbing, higher and higher,
The branches blow and I see a spire,

The gleam of a turret, the glint of a dome,

All sparkling and bright, like white sea foam.

On and on, from bough to bough,
The leaves are thick, but I push my way through;

Before, I have always had to stop
But to-day I am sure I shall reach the top.

Today to the end of the marvelous stair,
Where those glittering pinacles flash in the air!

Climbing, climbing, higher I go,

With the sky close above me, the earth far below.

Edited by Kate Riggs ~ Designed by Rita Marshall ~ Published in 2026 by Creative Editions
P. O. Box 227, Mankato, MN 56002 USA ~ Creative Editions is an imprint of The Creative Company
www.thecreativecompany.us ~ Printed in China
Library of Congress Cataloging-in-Publication Data
Names: Lowell, Amy, 1874-1925 author | Domeniconi, Paolo illustrator ~ Title: Climbing / Amy Lowell ; illustrated by Paolo Domeniconi. ~ Description: Mankato, MN : Creative Editions, 2026. | Audience term: Children | Audience: Ages 6-9 | Audience: Grades 2-3 | Summary: In this illustrated poem symbolizing resilience, the narrator climbs an apple tree toward a distant, sparkling town, and, despite previous unsuccessful attempts, is now able to reach the top. ~ Identifiers: LCCN 2025015270 (print) | LCCN 2025015271 (ebook) | ISBN 9781568464213 hardcover | ISBN 9781568464220 ebook ~ Subjects: LCSH: Tree climbing—Juvenile poetry | Resilience (Personality ~ trait)—Juvenile poetry | Children's poetry, American | CYAC: Tree climbing—Poetry | Resilience—Poetry | American poetry | LCGFT: Poetry | Picture books ~ Classification: LCC PS3523.O88 C55 2026 (print) | LCC PS3523.O88 (ebook) | DDC 811/.52—dc23/eng/20250527 ~ LC record available at https://lccn.loc.gov/2025015270 ~ LC ebook record available at https://lccn.loc.gov/2025015271
First edition 9 8 7 6 5 4 3 2 1